A GIRLFRIEND'S FINANCIAL SURVIVAL GUIDE

IT SHOULDN'T BE THAT HARD

Elana Milianta, CRPC®, CDFA®, AIF™

ARCHWAY
PUBLISHING

Archway Publishing books may be ordered
through booksellers or by contacting:

Archway Publishing
1663 Liberty Drive
Bloomington, IN 47403
www.archwaypublishing.com
844-669-3957

ISBN: 978-1-6657-1027-5 (sc)
ISBN: 978-1-6657-1028-2 (e)

Library of Congress Control Number: 2021915300

Print information available on the last page.

Archway Publishing rev. date: 9/24/2021

Written from the heart with humor and emotional honesty, this book will take readers on the journey of their lifetime, empowering women and giving them the tools to live the best life they can financially.

ACKNOWLEDGEMENTS

Thank you to my husband Chris, who motivated me to pursue my passions and tirelessly supported me along the way. Thank you to my children, Michael, Taylor and Justin. My hope is this book will serve as a reminder of the lesson that anything is possible with hard work and perseverance. To my stepchildren, Reese, Asia, and Kaya, thank you for completing our family. You are all a source of motivation to do better as a mother and a woman inspiring other women. Thank you to my sister, Yana, who continues to encourage me to block out the noise, and always keep going. To my tribe of women; Ellen, Deb, and Jennifer, thank you for your inspiration and support along this journey and the joy our friendship brings each decade of our lives.

This book is dedicated to my parents, Valentina and Ilia, who came to this country to build a better life for their children. This book would not be possible without their inspiration, and their commitment to the American dream.

DISCLOSURE

The information contained in this book does not purport to be a complete description of the securities, markets, or developments referred to in this material. The information has been obtained from sources considered to be reliable, but we do not guarantee that the foregoing material is accurate and complete. Any information is not a complete summary or statement of all available data necessary for making investment decisions and does not constitute a recommendation. All opinions are those of the author, and no one else. Expressions of opinion are as of the initial book publishing date and are subject to change without notice.

The author is not responsible for the consequences of any particular transaction or investment decision based on the content of the book. All financial, retirement, and estate planning should be individualized as each person's situation is unique.

This information is not intended as a solicitation or an offer to buy or sell any security referred to herein. Keep in mind that there is no assurance that our recommendations or strategies will ultimately be successful or profitable, nor protect against a loss. There may also be the potential for missed growth opportunities that may occur after the sale of an investment. Recommendations, specific investments, or strategies discussed may not be suitable for all investors. Past performance may not be indicative of future results. You should discuss any tax or legal matters with the appropriate professional.

Examples throughout the book are not to be taken as advice. They are used for illustrative purposes only.

CONTENTS

INTRODUCTION

I wrote this book because I remember how difficult it was to make ends meet and just try to get ahead to build financial stability. When you add in; not having the tools or guidance to build a financial future, it makes it that much harder to know where to start from.

I came to the United States as an immigrant in 1979. My parents did not speak the language, and they only had $500 in their pocket. I remember that we moved into a two-bedroom apartment in the Bronx with four adults and four children. I saw what it takes to build financial stability from the struggles and determination of my parents.

My parents scrubbed floors for three dollars an hour until they saved up enough to get our own apartment. After hours and hours of learning the English language and working endless hours toward building a life for my sister and me, my parents eventually ended up saving enough and going into business for themselves. They showed us what it takes to build the "American Dream."

Throughout my childhood, my parents weren't around that much. They worked insane hours, and my sister, who is seven years older than I am, pretty much raised me. We were never really given the tools or guidance to learn how to budget and invest. The only thing I was ever taught is that if you wanted to build financial stability, you work, work, and work some more, which is pretty much what I have done my whole life, work.

But there is a much smarter way of doing it. When I started

in this career, I had to just trust in myself and take a leap of faith. The survival rate in the financial services industry is about 12 percent. If you add in being a woman in this industry, the survival rate goes down even more so. But I was so passionate about this business and absolutely loved helping others work toward financial independence that I put all my blood, sweat, and tears into my career.

As I continued my own journey as a single woman and then wife, mom, and divorced woman, I realized that if I weren't in this career, I might have been on the other side where I see a lot of my friends and clients are before they come to me. I can understand why they find finances confusing and sometimes intimidating. That's why it was so important for me to write this book. It doesn't matter where you are in life, if you are just starting out or somewhere in the middle.

This book is about giving you an understanding of the different tools out there and a guide to help you through your life's journey. I'm here to educate you on what you need to be thinking about and help you work toward it.

STAGE 1

Man, I Feel Like a Woman

#Adulting

CHAPTER ONE

Kiss Starbucks Goodbye

Eat in or out?

Gucci or Targét?

Need or want?

My sixteen-year-old daughter Taylor is now home with me every day while I work and she is doing her virtual school. And if anyone has a teenage daughter, I'm sure you deal with the following daily.

"Mom, I need my grande vanilla sweet-cream cold brew!"

"Mom, there is nothing to eat!"

This demand for Starbucks coffee every morning and Uber Eats in the afternoon is enough to make anyone go broke ... or insane, to say the least. Being the financial person that I am, I've started doing the numbers for her.

"Do you know that instead of spending ten dollars a day on random, unnecessary high-caloric drinks and foods, you could take that money, invest it, earn a 6 percent compounded rate of return, and have over a million dollars by the time you retire at age sixty-five?"

Her response is, "Blah, blah, blah, blah. I want my Starbucks!"

It is pretty mind-boggling, right? But it's relatively simple. However, most of us do not think in those terms, especially teenagers. However, as you start approaching the #adulting stage, you need to start thinking about it.

Rate of Return Comparison

DISCLOSURE

This is a hypothetical illustration and not intended to reflect the actual performance of any particular security. Future performance cannot be guaranteed, and investment yields will fluctuate with market conditions.

So where do we start, and how do we do it?
It's amazing what the power of budgeting can do for your

finances. It almost sounds too simple; however, most people have no idea how much is coming into the household and how much is leaving. Do you know what you are spending on? Have you ever just sat down and did a breakdown of every purchase? I would guess that most would say no.

The easiest way to set a budget for yourself is to know how much money is coming in and going out. First, create two columns: fixed expenses and discretionary expenses. Or to simplify it, break down your spending between needs and wants.

Fixed expenses include things that are necessities such as housing, food, transportation, and clothing. And no, ladies, not your Gucci. Just the basics.

Discretionary expenses include things like entertainment, vacations, hobbies, or your bag of tricks to maintain your youthfulness. I like to call it "me maintenance." You'll want to be sure to include out-of-pattern expenses (e.g., holiday gifts, car maintenance, and home repairs) in your budget as well. I'm also very aware as a woman who gets her needs (hair, nails, and feet) done that those expenses naturally flow to the fixed expenses. Kidding, but not kidding.

To make sure you are not forgetting anything, it may help to look through your bank statements, credit card bills, and other receipts from the past year. Finally, as you list your expenses, it is important to remember your financial goals. Whenever possible, treat your goals as expenses and contribute toward them regularly.

As you establish your budget, you should examine your financial goals. Start by making a list of your short-term goals (e.g., new car or vacation) and long-term goals (e.g., purchasing a home, a child's education, retirement, or "me maintenance").

Next, ask yourself, "How important is it for me to achieve this goal? How much will I need to save?" Equipped with a clear vision of your priorities, you will work to build a budget that will help you achieve them.

Compare the two totals once you have added up your income and expenses. You should spend less than what is coming in so you can stay ahead. You're on the right track if your income column is greater than your expense column. If it is not, then look closely at your expenses and reduce your discretionary spending. Don't panic if you find yourself coming up short! All it's going to take is some persistence and a little self-discipline, and you'll get it right eventually. You may need to regularly review your budget and make adjustments. Here are a few tips to help keep you on track.

- Agree on a budget up front and check your progress quarterly or annually.
- Stay disciplined. Try to make budgeting a part of your daily routine.
- Start your new budget at a time when it will be easy to follow and stick with the plan (beginning of the year as opposed to right before the holidays).
- Find a budgeting system that fits your needs. (There are a ton of budgeting apps.)
- Distinguish between expenses that are wants (e.g., designer shoes) and expenses that are needs (e.g., groceries).
- Build rewards into your budget. I set up a fun fund for myself, which allows me to spend on my wants without feeling guilty.
- Avoid using credit cards to pay for everyday expenses. It may seem like you're spending less, but your credit card debt will continue to increase.

Last thought—skip the cups and save the buck$!

CHAPTER TWO

Sock It Away

I know I put it somewhere ...

Needs and wants

Dream vacation

When you have teenagers, you just never know when you need cash, so I always like to have it on hand, plus a little extra for emergencies. I tend to hide it because I have six kids and all their friends are constantly in and out of the house.

Do you ever hide your cash in random places thinking, *What a great spot!* But somehow when you need it, you forget where you put it? You start searching all your drawers. Underwear drawer—nope. T-shirt drawer—nope. Sock drawer—nope.

How about we put it away in a place where we always know where it is and, most importantly, where it is growing. We do not want it mixed in with those forever mysterious missing socks. All kidding aside, when I talk about "sock it away," of course I am referring to saving and investing. The questions are when, where, and how.

When?

The minute you start making money, start with paying yourself first. After you have covered all your fixed expenses, create savings buckets for yourself. Start with a rainy day fund. Purple rain, purple rain ...nope, it has nothing to do with Prince. This is your emergency fund, which should be your most liquid assets. Preferably three to six months of expenses should be put away in a separate savings or bank account used to cover or offset the costs of unforeseen situations.

The goal is to tap your emergency savings only for expenses directly related to an unforeseen emergency. You would know how much to build up to by setting a goal for a specific dollar amount for that bucket. When you draw from the emergency savings, you'll know how much to contribute in order to re-plenish the account. And it is important to always restore it to its original amount when you take money from this account.

Your next bucket for savings is your short-term bucket, which is for the goals you have five years or less to plan for. I maintain this bucket for my home projects. This bucket was my saving grace when COVID-19 hit and I was stuck working from home with six kids. It was summer 2020 with nowhere to go. My pool club and my gym were both closed. The two things I love most, working on my beach body and going to show it off at my pool club (not really, but it sounded good) were suddenly torn out of my life. So, I decided to convert my storage room to a gym and build a pool in my backyard. It's not exactly the same atmosphere I am used to. I no longer have fellow gym members to entertain me while working out, just the boilers in my storage room. To make matters worse, I am no longer being served my favorite cocktails at the pool, but that's OK. After all, it is a pandemic. I digress. I was daydreaming of what life used to be like. Now back to savings.

Always have funds for that one- to five-year horizon. You never know when a pandemic will hit and you'll be locked in your house with nowhere to go, so you need to start some major renovations to turn your home into an office/gym/spa/

restaurant/nail salon/school/bar/nightclub. If it is less than five years, you want your money to grow conservatively, and you want to have liquidity.

Next on the list are your five- to ten-year goals. This is your intermediate bucket. Your intermediate goals may consist of buying a home, car, business, or even the vacation home you've always wanted.

This bucket should still have liquidity but can be broken down between your more conservative investments, such as cash alternatives and bonds and more growth-oriented investments, such as stocks. (Stocks and bonds can also come in the form of mutual funds and index funds.)

Your last bucket will consist of your long-term goals, such as retirement or college savings for your kids. If your goals are more than ten years away, then this is your most aggressive bucket; this bucket can withstand the most volatility. Depending on your age and comfort, it makes sense to look into investments with the most growth potential, such as stocks.

Where?

Regardless of your financial goals, you'll need to decide how to best allocate your investment dollars. One important consideration is your risk tolerance. All investments involve some sort of risk, but a few involve more than others. How well can you handle the market's ups and downs? Are you willing to accept a higher degree of risk in exchange for the opportunity to earn a higher rate of return? Your answers to these questions will determine the right mix of cash, stocks, and bonds.

Whether you're investing for a new home, education, retirement, or any other financial goal, your overall objective is to maximize returns without taking on more risk than you can bear. But no matter what level of risk you are comfortable with, it is important that you choose investments that are consistent with your goals and time horizon. A financial advisor can help determine the most appropriate mix based on your goals and objectives.

How?

If you're not sure how much you should be saving every month, aim for a 20 percent rule of thumb. According to the popular 50/30/20 rule, you should reserve 50 percent of your budget for essentials like housing and food, 30 percent for discretionary spending like girls' night out (GNO), and travel. Don't forget "me maintenance", and, most importantly, at least 20 percent for savings.

The best way to start investing for your goals is first to set up an account for each bucket. Make sure you create your one- to five-year, five- to ten-year, and ten years-plus. Then automate your contributions into the appropriate buckets. When you automate these contributions, it's out of sight, out of mind. If you don't see it, you won't miss it. In turn, you will be making money while you sleep.

CHAPTER THREE

Ditch the Piggy Bank and Invest

What do I invest in?

What's the difference between IRA and 401(k)?

Stocks, bonds, mutual funds, and index funds— my head is spinning!

"When I save, it all goes into a bank account." Hmm. That may seem like a good idea to you, but it's not. How much is that savings paying you these days? These days, that savings rate can hardly keep up with inflation.

Don't get me wrong. Both savings and investing are important, but they are not the same thing. As I mentioned previously, savings are good for your emergency fund and your shorter-term bucket. However, once you have longer-term goals such as saving for your children's education or retirement, then you will have to start thinking about different investment vehicles.

How do you know what to invest in? You hear all these financial terms being thrown around, and I understand it can be very confusing and quite frankly overwhelming, but we are here to learn and not quit, so I am going to simplify it for you.

Many times, I hear, "I want to invest in an IRA."

To clarify, an individual retirement account (IRA) and a 401(k) are just retirement vehicles to hold the investments, such as stocks, bonds, and mutual funds. To break it down further, imagine the IRA and 401(k) as a car and the stocks, bonds, and mutual funds as the people in the vehicle.

To start off, these types of vehicles are typically used for retirement savings because they grow tax-deferred. What does that mean? Tax deferral is the process of delaying (but not necessarily eliminating) the payment of income taxes on income you earn in the current year. For example, the money you put into your traditional IRA or 401(k) retirement account isn't taxed until you withdraw it, which might be thirty or forty years down the road.

Tax deferral can be beneficial because:

- The money you would have spent on taxes remains invested.
- You may be in a lower tax bracket when you make withdrawals from your accounts (e.g., when you're retired).
- You can accumulate more dollars in your account due to compounding.

Think of compounding as the "rolling snowball" effect. Simply put, compounding pays earnings on your reinvested earnings.

Now let's talk about those pretty, little vehicles, ladies. Maserati, Porsche, or Mercedes, any takers? Okay, the vehicles

I am going to describe are not quite as exciting as those. But if you start putting money away now and investing and planning for those goals, then that pretty, little vehicle may be in your future if you plan wisely.

One of the best ways to accumulate funds for retirement or any other investment objectives is to use tax-advantaged (i.e., tax-deferred or tax-free) savings vehicles when appropriate.

Note, these contribution limits are for 2021.

- **Traditional IRAs:** Anyone who earns income or is married to someone with earned income—ladies, even if you are the chief family officer (CFO) of your family and your job does not produce income for you—you still contribute to an IRA. Depending upon your income and whether you're covered by an employer-sponsored retirement plan, you may or may not be able to deduct your contributions to a traditional IRA, but your contributions always grow tax-deferred. However, you'll owe income taxes when you make a withdrawal. Contributions are $6,000 with an additional $1,000 for a catch-up if you are over fifty.

- **Roth IRAs:** Roth IRAs are open only to individuals with income below certain limits. Your contributions are made with after-tax dollars but will grow tax-deferred, and qualified distributions will be tax-free when you withdraw them. The amount you can contribute is the same as for traditional IRAs.

- **Savings Incentive Match Plan for Employees: SIMPLE IRAs and SIMPLE 401(k):** These plans are generally associated with small businesses. As with traditional IRAs, your contributions grow tax-deferred, but you'll owe income taxes when you make a withdrawal. A SIMPLE IRA allows both the employee and small business owner or sole proprietor to make contributions. Contributions are $13,500 with a catch-up of $3,000 for individuals fifty and older.

- **Simplified Employee Pension (SEP) IRA:** Also used for small businesses, however with a SEP versus a SIMPLE, contributions are made by the employer only for themselves and their employees. Contribution limits are 25 percent of salary or up to $57,000, depending on which is less.
- **Employer-sponsored plans [401(k), 403(b), 457 plans]:** Contributions to these types of plans grow tax-deferred, but you'll owe income taxes when you make a withdrawal. You can contribute up to $19,500 for 2021 to one of these plans. Individuals age fifty and over can contribute an additional $6,500 for 2021. Employers can generally allow employees to make after-tax Roth contributions, in which case qualifying distributions will be tax-free.

Ladies, if you work for a company and they offer an employer-sponsored plan, check if they match your contribution. Basically that is free money in your pocket. And who doesn't like free?

Let's bring our attention to the people in the car. Those are the investments. The most common investments you will hear about are stocks, bonds, mutual funds, and index funds. Since we are going with the whole car analogy, let's take a road trip with your besties (i.e., investments).

Samantha *Stock – aka Equities*

She's the fun and exciting one. She's the one everyone is always talking about.

So what is a stock? Companies sell shares of stock to investors as a way to raise money to finance expansion, pay off debt, and provide capital. Each share of stock represents a share of ownership in the company. When you buy shares of a company, you then become a holder of the stock. As the stock grows, your money grows as well.

But keep in mind that the same way it goes up, in times it will go down too.

The main reason that investors buy stock is to seek capital appreciation and growth. Although past performance is no guarantee of future results, stocks have historically provided a higher average annual rate of return over long periods of time than other investments, including bonds and cash alternatives.

Charlotte *(Bond)* - *aka Fixed Income*

She's the conservative and quiet one. Not as exciting as Samantha Stock, a little boring at times, but they are your go to in times of uncertainty. The way we invest in a bond is to think about it as an IOU.

Governments and corporations commonly use bonds in order to borrow money. By you purchasing a bond, you assume the role of a lender and are lending your money to the corporation or government. And in turn, they are paying you interest for allowing them to borrow the funds from you.

At times, depending on who the issuer is, such as the government, those interest payments to you can be tax-free income, which means you do not pay income taxes on those earnings. So depending on where you fall in the tax bracket, sometimes it is more advantageous to go with tax-free income versus taxable or sometimes vice versa. It is always best to speak to your accountant and financial advisor to determine which investment makes the most sense.

It is also important to understand that all investments come with different levels of risk. Bonds are typically (not always) more conservative than stocks and in turn historically have provided a lesser return over the long term.

Carrie *(Mutual Fund)*

So we all have that friend that has her collection of designer shoes; Louboutin's, YSL, Jimmy Choo's. If you pack all those shoes (stocks, bond, etc.) in your one fancy bag, that is your mutual fund.

The technical meaning is a professionally managed investment that pools money from many investors to purchase a *collection* of securities like stocks, bonds, money market instruments, and other assets.

All you need to know is when you purchase a mutual fund, which is your fancy bag, inside are a bunch a different shoes; which are your securities, whether it be stocks, bonds, money markets, or a combination of the latter. That's like finding gold. How do I get a bag like that?

Within actively managed mutual funds, the decisions to buy and sell securities are made by one or more portfolio managers, supported by a team of researchers. You do not pick the individual securities; the managers do. In turn, the mutual fund investors do not actually own the securities in which the fund invests; they only own the shares in the fund itself.

Buying shares in a mutual fund is also an easy way to help diversify your investments, which is really another way of saying that you won't have all your eggs in one basket. One mutual fund can hold more than a hundred securities. Now that's a lot of shoes. Every girls dream, isn't it?

Index Funds

Similar to mutual funds, index funds are a *collection* of securities (stocks and bonds) wrapped up in one fund. But here's the biggest distinction: index funds invest in a specific list of securities (e.g., stocks of the S&P 500-listed companies only), while active mutual funds invest in a changing list of securities, chosen by an investment manager.

In addition, index funds seek market-average returns, while

active mutual funds try to outperform the market. Typically active mutual funds have higher fees than index funds. One is not better than the other. They serve different purposes within your investments. It's best to hire a professional that can guide you in what makes the most sense for your investment strategy.

The next time the market has a severe pullback, these are some fun and interesting facts to refer back to.

- Pullbacks of 10 percent are normal. On average, stock market corrections happen every two years. (Yardeni.com)
- A stock market correction is a market decline between 10 and 19 percent.
- Corrections are least likely in the third year of a presidential term. (Yardeni.com)
- There have been eighteen economic recessions in the past hundred years, averaging one every five and a half years. (Liberated Stock Trader)
- The following are stock market correction statistics (Seeking Alpha)
    o On any given day, stocks have roughly a 53 percent chance of rising and a 47 percent chance of falling.
    o Over any given three-month period, stocks rise 68 percent of the time, dropping the other 32 percent of the time.
    o Over a typical twelve-month period, the odds of making money in stocks rise roughly 75 percent.
    o If you are in the market for a long enough period of time, there is a 100 percent chance that you will experience temporary price declines at times.
- From 1980 to 2019, the S&P 500 index posted an average annual return of 11.8 percent. (Lord Abbett)
    - In the last twenty years (2000 to 2020), we have had only two (2000 to 2002 and 2007 to 2009) recessions until the short-lived Coronavirus one. (Wikipedia)

- October is the most volatile month, and September is the worst month when it comes to returns.
- Stock market declines of 5 to 10 percent generally require a month's recovery time. (Guggenheim Investments)
- "The Dow" isn't what you probably think. Most people think it is a representation of the whole market. The Dow stock index is made up of just thirty companies.

DISCLOSURE

The S&P 500 is an unmanaged index of five hundred widely held stocks that is generally considered representative of the U.S. stock market.

The Dow Jones Industrial Average (DJIA), commonly known as "The Dow," is an index representing thirty stocks of companies maintained and reviewed by the editors of the Wall Street Journal.

Indices are not available for direct investment. Any investor who attempts to mimic the performance of an index would incur fees and expenses, which would reduce returns.

Every type of investment, including mutual funds and index funds, involves risk. Risk refers to the possibility that you will lose money (both principal and earnings) or fail to make money on an investment. Changing market conditions can create fluctuations in the value of an investment. In addition, there are fees and expenses associated with investing in mutual and index funds that do not usually occur when purchasing individual securities directly.

Investors should carefully consider the investment objectives, risks, charges, and expenses of an investment company before investing. The prospectus contains this and other information and should be read carefully before investing. The prospectus is available from your investment professional.

401(k) plans are long-term retirement savings vehicles.

Withdrawal of pre-tax contributions and/or earnings will be subject to ordinary income tax and, if taken prior to age 59.5, may be subject to a 10 percent federal tax penalty.

Matching contributions from your employer may be subject to a vesting schedule. Please consult with your financial advisor for more information.

Contributions to a traditional IRA may be tax-deductible depending on the taxpayer's income, tax-filing status, and other factors. Withdrawal of pre-tax contributions and/or earnings will be subject to ordinary income tax and, if taken prior to age fifty-nine and a half, may be subject to a 10 percent federal tax penalty.

Roth IRA owners must be fifty-nine and a half or older and have held the IRA for five years before tax-free withdrawals are permitted.

CHAPTER FOUR

Dig Out of Debt

Where do I even start?

I feel like I am drowning with all this debt.

How can I get my credit score up?

Do you ever get on your scale and then step off just to move it to a different spot and then get back on to see if the number miraculously went down? I do. It doesn't. It's a shame. If it were different times, I may want to focus on that number a little more, but with my new added COVID weight, I won't.

The number I want to focus on is your credit score, the number you never want to go down, the number you always need to pay close attention to and work on. The higher it is, the better.

Debt could sometimes equate to good debt, but often times when we talk about debt, we are referring to bad debt.

I remember my first year in college, in the hub where all the kids would gather, a bunch of credit card vendors were just eager to have us sign up. Little did I know the damage it could do, especially as an eighteen-year-old having no experience with credit cards. By the time I was done with college, I was in over my head with debt.

To tackle debt, the first thing I learned is that you need to change the behavior that got you into this in the first place. I feel like, as women, we are victims to retail therapy. At least I know I am. The best thing you can do is admit and face it head-on. "I am a shopaholic. I am a shopaholic." That feels better already, doesn't it?

Next, make a list of everything you value in your life and then list everything you spent money on this past month. If the lists do not match, then work on getting your spending in line with your values. Start in baby steps, as it can get extremely overwhelming. I did it, and you can do it too.

First, start by cutting up the cards that got you into this situation in the first place. Next, list every credit card you have, the balance you owe, and the interest you are paying on it.

Evaluate Your Options

You may want to look at some zero percent balance-transfer credit cards. Those could provide immediate relief for those high annual percentage rate (APR) credit cards. Keep in mind that you need good credit to get approved for a new credit card, and if the balances are too high, you may be denied. Also more credit means more temptation to spend. So ladies, please be mindful of that.

Another option you could look into is consolidating your credit card debt with an unsecured personal loan. If you are going this route, make sure the interest rate payment is less than you are currently paying. And you still need good credit to get a personal loan, but it may be easier than getting another credit card. Going to a local bank or credit union would be your first stop to help you with a personal loan.

Pay Off Your Most Expensive Debts First

Choose the one debt charging you the most interest and focus all your extra payments on paying off that one first. Once you have paid that one off, focus on paying the next most expensive debt. Making extra payments each month can also lower your credit utilization ratio, which in turn can improve your credit score.

Keep in mind, if you are going through some sort of hardship, reach out to the credit card companies. Many times they will work out a payment plan with you. They'd rather get paid than not.

As you are paying off your debt, set yourself a spending allowance, but first you must go through your expenses and understand how much you are bringing in and what your cost of living is. And remember as we discussed previously, break it down between your fixed (needs) and your discretionary (wants) expenses.

People often ask, "What do I do first: pay down debt or save?"

The first thing to do is pay down bad debt first and then save. The easiest way to think about savings versus paying down debt is how much is it costing you to carry that debt (i.e., you are paying 20 percent interest on your card) versus how much you are making on your money (i.e., earning 0.05 percent in a savings account or 7 percent in a brokerage account). Your debt is costing more than you are making, so pay it off first.

Discipline yourself by setting up a budget for your discretionary spending. Many times it helps using cash because it is easier to keep track of instead of credit. Pull out the cash at the beginning of the month that you have allocated for your fun fund, and as soon as you go through that cash, it means you need to stop spending.

Who am I kidding? Who's using cash these days? Who's even going out these days? We are all sitting on the couch ordering from Amazon. Did I mention TikTok? I now have every organization gadget, cleaning product, and Lulu legging dupe out there. Of course, having these products at the click of a button makes it all too easy. I'm guilty myself. It's no wonder we are racking up debt.

I know. It's so much fun to get a package every day. It's our only form of entertainment. I get it. Do you ever get a package and forget you ordered it? I think it's happening more and more these days. Blame it on the wine or the boredom. You can continue to blame and make excuses, but that's not going to bring you financial independence, ladies.

Oh, don't forget all those subscriptions: FabFit, Ipsy, Date Box, and you name it. They seem to have a box for everything these days. I even found a wine subscription. I bet they are doing really well. Hey, stop searching ladies! We are not looking to add additional subscriptions, and just to remind you, wine o'clock is 5PM again!

So how do we get our binge spending under control? I created a whole separate checking account for my fun fund. This way I have a debit card and transfer a certain amount every month that I set up in my budget for my fun spending. Once I have depleted those funds, I'm done spending. It's that easy!

Every month, I also open up my apps and see what subscriptions I am still paying for and if I still use them. Mine typically consists of some sort of dieting app. I am forever stepping on that scale and trying to make it move down. It's not, and it's very upsetting. I talk about discipline. I need to work on disciplining my mouth.

Back to the serious stuff again. Ever hear of the term *debt-to-income ratio*? This is a commonly used figure that puts your debt into perspective relative to how much money you make. This number is very important if making a home purchase is on your list of goals.

Banks look at this number to determine if they are willing to lend you money for a mortgage. Without getting too much into the weeds, the best way to describe this debt-to-income ratio is if you make $50,000 a year and you have $25,000 in debt, your debt ratio is 0.50. It is your monthly debt payments divided by your gross monthly income (consumerfinance.gov).

The maximum debt-to-income ratio that a homebuyer can have is 43 percent, if you want to take out a qualified mortgage (smartasset.com). Of course there will be lenders that will lend to individuals with higher debt-to-income, but keep in mind you may be paying a higher interest rate on that money.

I do want to add that these days' mortgages are so cheap that it is better to use the bank's money than your own. For example, if a mortgage is at a rate of 3.75 percent but the money is potentially earning in excess of 8 percent,[1] you're better off using the bank's money more so than the money invested. Of course it all comes back to what you can afford as a mortgage payment and many other variables that a financial advisor and mortgage consultant can walk you through.

However, the rule of thumb is that lenders typically want no more than 28 percent of your gross monthly income to go toward your monthly mortgage payment. For example, if you and your significant other make a combined gross income of $100,000, your annual mortgage payment should not exceed $28,000.

As we discuss debt, credit plays a big role in creating financial independence. First, you will want to avoid these credit traps. And because lenders, landlords, and others care how you handle your bills and other financial decisions, you will want to understand how to build credit and maintain it at a superior level.

---

[1] This is a hypothetical example for illustration purpose only and does not represent an actual investment or mortgage loan rate.

To calculate your credit score, companies first pull information from your credit report such as how much money you owe, whether you have paid on time or late, how long you've had credit, how much new credit you have, and whether you asked for new credit recently (consumer.ftc.gov).

Then companies compare that information to the credit behavior of people with similar profiles. Based on this comparison, you get assigned a score, typically between 300 and 850. A higher score means better credit. According to Equifax, generally credit scores from 580 to 669 are considered fair, 670 to 739 are considered good, 740 to 799 are considered very good, and 800 and up are considered excellent.

Make yourself credit-savvy with these few tips:

- TransUnion, Equifax, and Experian are the three reporting agencies you need to know about.
- Be sure to make payments on time; otherwise it could negatively affect your credit report.
- Do not use more than 30 percent of available revolving balance (the amount of money credit card companies are allowing you to borrow); any more than that can negatively impact your credit score.
- When using revolving credit, avoid spending more than you can pay off at the end of each billing cycle.
- Be aware of hidden interest and fees.
- When transferring balances to take advantage of low interest rates, be sure to pay off the outstanding balances before the teaser rate expires.
- Many times when lenders offer very low introductory rates, these rates generally last no more than three to six months and increase to the current market rate thereafter that can be in excess of 20 percent. Moreover, the introductory rates may apply only to balances you transfer from other cards. They may not apply to new purchases and rarely, if ever, to cash advances. Finally, if your monthly payment is late, the

interest rate may be raised to the current market rate and sometimes beyond.

- Closing an account might hurt your score rather than help.
- When you pay off balances, your credit score should go up.
- Your FICO credit score likes when you have a variety of debt such as mortgage, auto, and credit card, and when they see that you are paying down all that debt in a timely manner, that helps improve your overall score.

Well, there you have it. Before you know it, if you continue with this strategy, you will most likely start seeing your debt go down and credit score go up, and you will feel so much better knowing that you are making strides to living the financial dream and building toward your financial independence.

DISCLOSURE

Please seek the assistance of a mortgage professional.

CHAPTER FIVE

When You Need to Make a Choice

Discovering Yourself: Career, Business, and Family

Career or family?

Who am I?

Am I a grown-up yet?

In my last year and a half of college, I decided to go into business for myself. Yes, I know, crazy! What would possess me to open a business when I was still going to school full time? I don't know. I guess I just had all these big dreams. Throughout college, I worked for a children's boutique, and I loved all the little babies that would come in. I had so much fun dressing them up in all the cute clothing. One day the owner decided she needed to close her business because she had too much family stuff going on. So I thought to myself, *I can do this. Why not?*

I went to my mom and told her how Vivian was going out of business and I wanted to open my own children's boutique. She told me she had saved up money for my wedding and if I wanted to use those funds, I could have them. However, she said it was important that I had a financial stake in it as well.

For me, it was a no-brainer. I wasn't getting married anytime soon. So with the little I had saved up plus the additional funds from my mom, I opened my very own business, Children's Classics. I knew I had a lot to learn, but I was so young and hungry to succeed that I jumped in and took a chance.

As I continued to work on my bachelor's degree, my grades started to slip. Needless to say, it was quite a bit of a juggling act to run a business and go to school full time. Finally the time came where I needed to decide. I was approaching the end of my senior year, and I had to make a choice: either focus on the business or put my energy into learning a new craft. I couldn't do both. I was majoring in finance and international business, and an internship opened up at a financial firm. With a lot of going back and forth, I knew I had to take it.

Thank God for my sister, who was the chief family officer (CFO) of her home. She was taking some time off to enjoy motherhood and was able to help me out with my business.

As my sister continued managing my business and I was falling in love with the finance world, I had to make a decision whether to continue with my business journey or commit myself to taking on a brand-new career. I finally made up my mind and chose the world of finance, and my sister ended up purchasing the store from me. It was a win-win for both of us at the end.

My sister has always been a fashionista and found her passion with owning a retail store. I didn't know then, but I quickly found out how passionate I was about helping individuals and families with their financial future.

Whether you are starting a new career, changing careers, deciding to leave the workforce to work on your role as the CFO of your household, or opening your own business, they are all big decisions, and they are financial decisions you need to make and plan for ahead.

Going into my own retail business at a very young age, becoming a mom, shifting careers, and building a financial advisory practice over the past twenty years has taught me quite a bit, and I'm still learning until this day.

I wouldn't be up-front if I didn't admit to being scared at times, questioning whether I made the right decision and feeling guilty that I chose a career over staying at home with my kids. I think, as women, sometimes we lose ourselves.

What I did learn is that we do have a lot more options these days. I also don't think we need to make a choice between career and family anymore. I've learned you can do both, if that is what you choose. I think if this pandemic has taught us anything, we can work from home, get creative, be productive, and still take care of our family.

Many times we also sacrifice our well-being for others' well-being. Sometimes we have a choice; other times we do not. Whatever the circumstance is, it is important to take care of yourself. I know, as women, we forget that sometimes.

These days I think everyone is trying to re-create themselves. If there is one good thing about COVID, it has certainly provided a lot of quiet time where we can actually take a step back and reassess—reassess us as individuals, our relationships, our goals, and our purpose. I would have to say, regardless if you are trying to create a new you or just improve on the already fabulous you, there is always room for improvement and growth.

As I sit here and write this, this chapter is becoming clearer and clearer to me. I guess the point I am trying to make is that I want to celebrate you, to celebrate us as moms, sisters, daughters, and friends.

We are all doing the best we can with what we have. It's our job to encourage and hold each other up. We all have a story, and we all have our inner battles. It is completely normal. Let's listen to each other, be compassionate, educate one another, and just share. You never know when your story can be someone's saving grace.

STAGE 2

I Do!

How to Handle Marriage, Motherhood, and Money

CHAPTER SIX

Before You Say "I Do"

Yes ...　　　No ...　　　Maybe so?

DISCLAIMER: Caution upon entering!

If you have come to terms that you will have someone who will be chewing in your ear the rest of your life, dropping little tiny hairs all over your bathroom sink, leaving dirty clothes by the bed, snoring and keeping you up for the next fifty years, and just annoying you forever and ever and you still love them, then you have met your happily-ever-after.

So let's plan for the big day! As little girls, I think we all dream about being that princess for the day: wedding dress, venue, guest list, invitations, band or DJ, chicken or fish, and so on. Decisions, decisions, decisions.

As wonderful as planning for this big day is, you'll want to think about how marriage will impact your financial situation. And while there are a number of issues you'll need to consider, careful planning can increase the likelihood that you'll have financial success as you enter this new chapter in your life.

Marriage is the union of two separate individuals and their

finances. While talking about money can be a stressful topic for many couples, you'll want to sit down and discuss both of your financial history before you merge your money.

Start by taking stock of each of your respective financial situations. You should each make a list of your individual assets (e.g., investments and real estate) and any debt (e.g., student loans and credit cards) that you may have.

Right now, you are probably accustomed to managing your finances in a way that is comfortable for you and you alone. Once you unite, you and your spouse will have to agree on a system for budgeting, paying your bills, and saving as a couple for your goals together.

Talking through what is important to you and understanding what money means to the both of you is the first step to planning for a successful marriage. If you have one person who is all about saving and the other is all about spending, this could become an issue down the line. Setting expectations now could save a lot of turmoil later, not to mention you won't have to hide all those packages when they come in.

An important part of planning as a couple is to map out your future together. Where do you see yourself a year and five years from now? Do you want to buy a home or rent? If you decide to start a family, does one spouse stay home while the other focuses on their career? Do you both work? What are your long-term career goals? Where do you see yourself making your home? These conversations are important to have to help you both start on the right path together.

Together you should make a list of short-term goals (e.g., paying off wedding debt or buying a home) and long-term goals (e.g., retirement). Prioritize what is most important to you and work toward them together by creating a budgeting and savings plan.

As you are creating your goals and working on a budgeting system together, this is also a good time to decide whether you and your future spouse will combine your bank accounts or keep them separate.

Since having good credit is an important part of any sound

financial plan, you'll want to identify any potential credit/debt problems either you or your spouse may have and work on resolving them now. To start your new chapter together on a new slate, pull your credit reports so there are no surprises. Regardless you should do this on an annual basis to make sure everything is up-to-date and accurate. (You can go to annual-creditreport.com.)

For the most part, you are not responsible for your future spouse's past credit problems, but they can prevent you from getting credit together as a couple after you are married. Even if you've always had perfect credit, you may be turned down for credit cards or loans that you apply for together if your future spouse has a bad track record with creditors. If that is the case, consider keeping your credit separate until you and your future spouse's credit improves.

If you are both working and entitled to health benefits, now is a good time to compare and do a cost/health benefits analysis and determine which plan both of you should go under. You'll also want to compare the premiums for one family plan against the cost of two single plans. Compare deductibles, co-payments, and overall benefits.

In addition, if both of you participate in an employer-sponsored retirement plan, you should review the plan's options. Plans may differ as to matching contributions, investment options, and loan provisions. If you can both afford to participate, max out your contribution in your own plan. If you cannot afford to do the maximum allowable contribution to both, look to compare who may have the better retirement plan options. Also keep in mind even if one spouse does not have a retirement plan or decides to stay home to raise the family, they are still entitled to have an IRA, which they can contribute and save toward retirement as well. Speaking with a professional can help you understand your choices, and which makes the most sense for your financial situation.

I know right now you are in a state of bliss. However, even if you never thought about signing a prenuptial agreement, it is wise to consider. If either you or your future spouse has or may inherit substantial assets or if either of you have children from previous marriages, this may protect you in the future. A prenuptial agreement is a contract a couple signs before they get married that sets forth the division of assets in the event of divorce or death.

A prenuptial agreement can ease your mind by spelling out what assets and liabilities each partner is bringing into the marriage and by determining how money or property brought into the marriage or acquired during the union will be divided if the marriage ends either in death or divorce.

A prenuptial agreement typically addresses the following areas:

- Assets and liabilities: What assets will each of you bring into the marriage? What liabilities do each of you have (e.g., credit card and mortgage debt)?
- Contributions of each partner: Will there be particular consideration given for special contributions that either of you makes (e.g., one spouse limiting their career)?
- Divorce: If you and your future spouse divorce, will there be alimony or a lump-sum payment? How will you divide assets from joint funds?
- Estate planning: Who gets what at the death of either spouse?

The most important lesson I can leave you with as you enter this new chapter of your journey is that it is so important that both spouses continue to partake in setting goals and working toward them together. Even if it is not a monetary contribution, your participation is key in developing a healthy balance with your spouse. Even if you are not the one responsible for paying the bills, you need to know what the bills are and how they are being paid.

True story, someone had her car repossessed because her husband stopped making lease payments on it. Somehow her husband, who was responsible for paying for the lease while she was caring for her sick parent in another state, mysteriously forgot to make the payments. She ended up coming home and finding a boot on her car. Since the lease was also in her name, her credit was ruined. Don't be oblivious.

You need to know what type of accounts you have and where they all are. Even if you are not interested, still participate in the meetings and understand how your money is being invested.

I only speak from experience, not only with my friends and family, but many of my clients as well. I constantly see women tend to take a back seat when it comes to finances. Don't! I get it. It may not be your forte; however, most of the time those stories don't typically end well.

And for the love of God, if you plan on filing your taxes together as a married couple, make sure you look through the tax return, speak with your accountant, and get an understanding of what you are signing. I cannot tell you how many times I come across my ladies and they tell me they never see the tax return and don't sign them, which means someone else is signing your signature.

Please, please, please do not have your spouse sign your tax return. Remember the New Jersey housewife? She had to serve time in jail because of some shady things her husband was doing. It happens. Do not put your head in the sand. It can come back and bite you in the ass.

Now on a brighter note, as you begin this new journey as a couple, here is a "Get Married" checklist to help you get started.

Get Married Checklist

Money Management

o   Have assets been itemized separately/together?   Y/N
o   Have debts been itemized separately/together?   Y/N
o   Have you determined who will be responsible for what expenses?   Y/N

o   Have separate/joint accounts been discussed?   Y/N

o   Will separate/joint checking/savings be used?   Y/N

o   Has a recordkeeping system been devised?   Y/N

o   Have you pulled credit reports?   Y/N

o   Are there any credit history concerns?   Y/N

Housing

o   Are you currently a homeowner?   Y/N

o   If not, is a home purchase in the plans?   Y/N

o   Have home ownership options been considered?   Y/N

o   Do you know your credit score?   Y/N

o   Do you know how much you can afford for a home?   Y/N

o   If not, have you hired a professional to help you with this?   Y/N

Insurance Planning

o   Is health insurance needed?   Y/N

o   Will separate health insurance plans be maintained?   Y/N

o   Will health coverage be combined?   Y/N

o   Does life insurance need to be purchased or upgraded?   Y/N

o   Does auto insurance need to be purchased or upgraded?   Y/N

o   Does homeowners/renters insurance need to be purchased/upgraded?   Y/N

o   Does disability income insurance need to be purchased/upgraded?   Y/N

o   Does personal liability (umbrella) need to be purchased/upgraded?   Y/N

o   Will beneficiary designations be changed?   Y/N

Investment Planning

o   Have investment goals been discussed and prioritized?   Y/N
o   Have separate/joint accounts been contemplated?   Y/N
o   Have you had each other's holdings assessed?   Y/N

Retirement Planning

o   Is a retirement plan available?   Y/N
   o   IRA   Y/N
   o   Employer-sponsored?   Y/N
o   If not, have they been set up?   Y/N
o   Will one or both plans be funded?   Y/N

Estate Planning

o   Is there a will?   Y/N
o   If so, will changes be made to the will?   Y/N
o   Is there a trust?   Y/N
o   Has setting up trusts been considered?   Y/N
o   Do you have durable power of attorneys set up?   Y/N
o   Have healthcare directives been established?   Y/N
o   Are spousal property transfers anticipated?   Y/N
o   Is there concern about equalizing estates?   Y/N

CHAPTER SEVEN

Welcome Home!

Am I dreaming?
Is this real?

Baby on board

Oy, I'm
exhausted!

DISCLAIMER: If children are not part of your plan, then go ahead and skip this chapter because you are already ahead of the game with your nest egg.

You spend your whole young adult life trying not to get pregnant, and then finally comes a time when your biological clock kicks in. And now you are doing everything possible to get pregnant. I remember those days.

I got married earlier than most. I was twenty-four, and even though I was still very early in my career and marriage, at twenty-five I just had this feeling that took over me that I wanted to start a family. And I tried and tried again, and nothing was working.

I set up an appointment with my OB/GYN, and when I arrived at her office, she walked me through a series of questions and tests. Before I knew it, I was sitting in a specialist's office, once again going through a series of tests.

I remember the day as if it were yesterday when I received

the call to come in and I was told the most dreadful news I could have ever imagined, "You can't conceive on your own." Obviously a wave of emotion overcame me. It was too much to digest right at that moment.

They told me I would need an egg donor because there was an issue with my eggs. After many tears and sleepless nights, I returned to the specialist, and this time, my mom and my sister joined me. He told me that since my sister has had babies and her DNA was 99 percent identical, she would be the perfect candidate to donate to me.

How is this even possible? I was only in my mid-twenties. How could I not be producing enough eggs?

My mother wasn't buying it. She said we would get a second opinion. Wiping away the tears and with her heavy Russian accent, she said, "You vill have yur babies. Don't you vorry." And I did. I had my babies.

After meeting with the second specialist, it was determined that my thyroid was off and causing all my numbers to be wacky. They put me on medication, and within a few months I was pregnant with my first baby. Blessed with a healthy little boy at age twenty-seven, I couldn't be more grateful.

Honestly, I think my first specialist was a scam artist. However, I was fortunate that my journey to motherhood didn't cost me an arm and a leg, which it certainly could have with the first doctor.

You never think that there could potentially be a problem. Why would you? But if growing your family is part of your bigger plan, then start saving now as much as you can.

As you become a mother, a whole other set of sacrifices set in. Oh, the joys of parenthood, which is certainly rewarding and can be frighteningly challenging at times. When you become a parent, the love that takes over you is like no love you can describe. It is the purest form of love. Children give gifts only a parent could understand, from those sticky little fingers on the walls to those sweet little kisses on your lips.

Children are your greatest responsibility as well as your biggest investment. So now that you have your little bundle of joy or planning for them, fast-forward. Let's take a look into your future.

Let me just tell you how expensive those little buggers are. From T-ball to ballet, Tae Kwon Do, gymnastics, driving lessons, and SAT tutors, it never ends! Don't forget to add the 50 Bar and Bat Mitzvah parties you should start saving for now. Oh, and those sweet sixteen parties, yeah, plan for those as well. As they are turning sixteen, you know what else they are expecting? Cars, not to mention top-of-the-line vehicles.

Yes, I had to work my ass off in order to get my first luxury car, and I was well into my thirties. These kids, nope, they want a BMW, Mercedes, or a pimped-out Jeep the minute they get their license. How about car insurance to cover a sixteen-year-old kid? It is insane!

I don't know. Back in the day, my first car was a hand-me-down gold, little hatchback Toyota Tercel. I named her Goldilocks. I thought I was hot shit and fabulous driving my little hatchback, no shame there!

You can't forget the biggest expense, education. Whether it be private or religious school, trade school or college. Educating your children is expensive, no matter which way you look at it.

So now, how do we save for your ballerina/karate kid/little gymnast? First, consider opening up a 529 for their education. A 529 is known as a qualified tuition plan. It allows you to save money for your child's education, and it grows federal tax-free. 529s were initially set up for college planning, but now you can use up to $10,000 in tax-free withdrawals for private, public, or religious K -12 (savingforcollege.com).

While plans can vary from state to state, about thirty states offer a tax credit or deduction for contributions into a 529 plan. It's important to understand that these state tax breaks are only available when the funds are withdrawn to pay for expenses that the state considers qualified, which may or may not include K-12 tuition.

Also, if the funds are withdrawn and not used for education, you'll pay regular tax as well as a 10 percent penalty. But if the goal is education savings, it's a beautiful thing when you let your money compound tax-free.

When opening a 529, you have options as to who can be the owner. A great option is to have a grandparent be the owner because colleges consider a 529 plan as part of your assets when considering financial aid. Also you can switch beneficiaries, so if one child doesn't use the funds, it can be transferred to another sibling.

A custodial account is a great savings vehicle for a child as well. Basically, you, the parent, are the custodian on the account for your child, who is the beneficiary. The custodian controls the account until your child reaches ages eighteen or twenty-one, depending on state laws.

These types of savings accounts are called Universal Gifts To Minors Act (UGMA) or Uniform Transfer Minors Act (UTMA). When I used to get cash gifts from friends and relatives for my kids, I would put half into their 529 and the other half into their custodial account.

Once my kids started to want to spend on little things for themselves, I got them a debit card tied to their custodial account and started teaching them about budgeting and saving. This account is also great for them to save for their goals, like their own car. I used this account to teach them money skills.

This account is not just for cash. You can also invest in stocks, bonds, and mutual funds as well. However, keep in mind, by eighteen or twenty-one, that account is 100 percent their own, which means they can spend however they would like and you have no say so. So be careful how much you allocate to this type of account. You don't want them turning twenty-one and now using all their funds on their beer pong weekends.

When your kids start to earn a little income, a Roth IRA is a great vehicle to set up for them. Some of the benefits are the money you contribute when you start to draw on them in retirement, minimum age is fifty-nine and a half, and the withdrawals are tax-free. Just think about all those years of compounding and growing, and when they start to use the funds, they don't pay taxes on all those earnings. That is amazing, and what a great vehicle to help them start building their own wealth.

Now keep in mind, your vehicle is the ROTH IRA (car). You need to invest in (all those people in the vehicle) stocks, bonds, and funds. You have to make sure that money doesn't sit in cash. I can't tell you how many times I see people who have these great retirement vehicles and all they are doing is sitting in cash. That is a very costly mistake. Please don't do that!

The other benefit is that you can use these funds for qualified education expenses without being penalized for withdrawing prior to age fifty-nine and a half. Contributions (but not earnings) can be withdrawn at any time, income tax- and penalty-free (Morningstar.com). So if you do not use these funds for educational purposes, you are giving them a head start in planning for their retirement.

If you have a special-needs baby, some of these vehicles could actually work against you if you rely on state and federal disability benefits. Saving money in the child's name can jeopardize those needs-based benefits. According to federal law, individuals lose eligibility to certain federal disability benefits if they have more than $2,000 in assets.

A tax-advantaged savings plan, Achieving a Better Life Experience (ABLE), was created to help families save in the name of their special-needs children without jeopardizing other critical financial benefits and programs that may be available to help their children. What's great about this vehicle is that after-tax contributions to these accounts grow tax-free as long as withdrawals are used for qualified disability expenses. And if you have an existing 529, you can now roll up to $15,000 per year into an ABLE account.

Before considering an ABLE account, you need to be aware of some drawbacks as well. Consulting with a specialist that deals with special needs can help you determine if this is the right vehicle for you.

Another savings vehicle for you to explore for a child with special needs is a Supplemental or Special Needs Trust. Money from an estate, life insurance, or other source can be deposited into a trust. The trust owns the assets, and the designated trustee controls how they are spent.

Trusts are the less restrictive option, but ABLE accounts are inexpensive, and you don't need an attorney to set it up for you. An added plus is that money withdrawn from ABLE accounts, as long as it is used for qualified expenses, is tax-free.

Allowable contributions will vary depending on the vehicle. A financial advisor, and accountant can provide you guidance.

Now you have the tools to start building a bright future for your little angel.

DISCLOSURE

CHAPTER EIGHT

Protect Yourself against the Unimaginable

Sudden illness

Loss of a loved one

Loss of income

Whether you are on this life journey solo or not, every woman needs to know how to protect herself and her family. I know it's difficult to think about the what-ifs in our life, such as losing a spouse, illness, accident, and so much more. However, planning for those what-ifs will protect us down the line from potentially having to deal with a financial catastrophe.

Regardless of age, wealth, or health, the first thing that everyone needs to do tomorrow morning, if you don't already have it in place, is to draw up four documents with an attorney.

A durable power of attorney (POA) lets you authorize someone to act on your behalf to handle your financial matters in the event you become physically or mentally unable to do so. The person you choose can do things like pay everyday expenses, watch over your investments, and file taxes.

Advanced medical directives let others know what medical

treatment you would want or not want in the event you can't express your wishes yourself. If you don't have an advanced medical directive, medical care providers must prolong your life using artificial means even if you do not want such procedures. There are different types of advanced medical directives. (Some states do not allow all types, so make sure you understand what is offered in your state.)

- A living will allows you to decline certain types of medical care even if you die as a result of that choice. In most states, living wills only take effect under certain circumstances, such as terminal illness.
- A do-not-resuscitate (DNR) is your directive to medical personnel to not perform CPR if you go into cardiac arrest.

A healthcare proxy appoints someone to make medical decisions for you in the event you are unable to do so for yourself.

A will is a legal document that sets forth your wishes regarding the distribution of your property and the care for any minor children after your death. If you die without a will, your wishes may not be carried out.

If you have minor children, you must appoint a guardian. If you don't have a guardian provision in your will, Child Protective Services may be brought in to care for your children should something happen to you. In addition, you will want to set up a trust for your minor children so your assets are distributed and used properly for the benefit of your children. You do not want your sixteen-year-old teenager inheriting all your assets outright and then going and partying it up, spending through everything you have ever worked for.

Many different types of trusts can be set up depending on your goals and objectives, and it is best to sit down with a trust and estate attorney to talk you through your options.

As a side note, if you have, for instance, your ex-spouse listed as your beneficiary on your retirement accounts, life insurance, or annuity, even if you listed someone else in your will for those assets, the beneficiary designation supersedes your will for those assets, which means your ex-spouse can potentially inherit those assets.

Now that you have the important documents in place, how do you protect yourself from a financial catastrophe? Insurance, insurance, and more insurance. The same way we have property insurance to protect our home and auto insurance to protect our cars, we need to protect ourselves from a financial catastrophe. What type of insurance is out there to protect us from income loss, disability, and accidents?

First, let's start with life insurance. Life insurance can protect you and your family from a loss of a loved one. When you are just starting a family, this is the first insurance you need to think about. There are three main types of insurance: term life, whole life, and universal life. There are many variations of each. Without getting too much in the weeds, what you'll need to know is:

- Term life is your least expensive and typically comes in ten-, fifteen-, twenty-, and thirty-year terms. If you do not pass away in the given term, you lose the death benefit (the amount paid out to your heirs upon passing). What I like about term is that if you are just starting out with a young family and can't really afford your permanent type of policies, then this is a good start in securing your family's finances.
- The next type you have probably heard about is whole life insurance, also known as "straight life" or "permanent life." This type of policy is known for its absolute guarantees, which means its promise to pay a death benefit if the premium has been paid. The three benefits with a whole life are a guaranteed rate of return on cash, a guaranteed cost that will not change and is locked in when you purchase, and a death benefit that is guaranteed to last for your "whole life."
- Universal life is a little more complex, with some additional bells and whistles. It is a form of permanent

life insurance with an investment savings element plus lower premiums than whole life. Unlike term life insurance, universal life can accumulate a cash value.

Because there are many variations of life insurance and they can be complex vehicles, it's best to sit down with a financial advisor and insurance specialist to determine which is the best fit for your situation.

Life insurance is a vehicle used to protect your family from the unthinkable, the loss of a loved one and their financial contribution to the family. But it can be used as an estate-planning tool as well. (That is a whole other book, but regardless a financial advisor and trust and estate attorney will help you figure out if that is a vehicle that would be appropriate for your family goals.)

How much life insurance is enough? Well, a bunch of factors needs to be taken into consideration when determining what enough is. Determine how long you will need the coverage. What type of costs do you want to cover with the life insurance? For instance, debt, income replacement, burial wishes, education for your children, and so forth. Everything that is important to you and has a dollar sign behind it, you should consider and then account for.

The other type of insurance you need to think about is disability insurance. This type of insurance replaces a portion of your monthly income if injury or illness prevents you from working. It provides financial security for you and your loved ones if you can no longer earn a paycheck.

Long-term care insurance, discussed in chapter 12, helps cover the cost of care when you have a chronic medical condition, disability, or disorder that would require you to either need assistance in your home or require you to go into a nursing home, assisted living facility, or adult day care center.

Lastly, an umbrella policy, which is relatively inexpensive, is designed to make sure you never find yourself living a nightmare. It is extra liability coverage in the event you are sued for more than what your existing insurance will pay. But if you ever did find yourself in that situation and you didn't have the extra coverage, you could potentially lose all your savings.

An umbrella policy will typically cover you in excess of regular homeowners, auto, or watercraft coverage. An additional benefit does not only cover the policy holder but also covers the members of the family and household. It covers injury to others as well as damage to their possessions.

I can't tell you how many times I come across individuals and families that have spent all their life saving and building up a nest egg but have nothing in place to protect that nest egg or their family.

I have just a few stories to share with you. I had a family friend. She was in her fifties, and her husband had developed Alzheimer's. She took care of him as long as she could until he eventually became violent and she had to put him in a home. Because she did not have long-term care insurance, she went through all her assets. By the time he passed away, she basically had nothing. Her three adult children now had to take care of their mother financially; otherwise she would have ended up on the street. This all could have been avoided if they planned properly and had long-term care insurance.

Another heart wrenching story was a case of a woman in her fifties as well. Her spouse, who was the provider, got ill and was no longer able to work. She had a job; however, it was not enough to cover their cost of living. Through the years, they went through all their savings. She was looking for a loan to help float their cost of living. But they were way in over their head with debt already because those were the means they were using to support their lifestyle. At that point, her credit was too poor as well. So a loan was not a possibility because of her debt-to-income ratio. If they had a disability policy, that might have helped their situation. At the end of the day, she wasn't left with many options.

The point is that you never want to be in a situation where it's too late. I can share another hundred different stories just like this. Stories like this can be avoided if you plan properly. Protect yourself, your family, and your nest egg!

DISCLOSURE

These policies have exclusions and/or limitations. The cost and availability of insurance depend on factors such as age, health, and the type and amount of insurance purchased. As with most financial decisions, there are expenses associated with the purchase of life insurance. Policies commonly have mortality and expense charges. In addition, if a policy is surrendered prematurely, there may be surrender charges and income tax implications. Guarantees are based on claims-paying ability of the insurance company.

CHAPTER NINE

Put Your Retirement First

Is it too late to start saving for retirement?

How much do I need to live comfortably in retirement?

How do I know if I have enough?

So you want to travel the world or maybe get that second home you have always dreamed of. However you envision your retirement, it will take work to build toward because these days you can spend as much time in retirement as you have spent working and accumulating your assets.

I'm a city girl now, but I've always wanted a farmhouse with a view of the mountains where my dogs could run around and play and I have my two rocking chairs on my porch watching all my grandbabies. That's my summer home. Then for the winters, I want to be a snowbird and head south to my beach home to relax on my deck overlooking the beautiful water. Ahh, that's a nice visual, isn't it? It beats the two feet of snow I am looking at right now and the thought of having to shovel it. Oy!

Yes, I have big dreams, and you can too. But you'd better start planning as early as possible since women face unique financial challenges. We tend to live longer, which means we need more money saved to carry us through retirement, and because we are living longer, we are also faced with more health care costs in retirement. If you add in career interruptions between raising children and caring for our elderly parents, there you have it. It affects our retirement benefits and Social Security.

So what do we need to know to get ahead of the game? You need to understand the different income sources used for retirement and how they work.

You must have worked for at least ten years to be entitled to your own Social Security benefits, and they are typically calculated on your best thirty-five years of earnings. But don't fret if you haven't worked and you were the CFO of your household. You can still qualify for benefits based on your spouse's or ex-spouse's earnings record. That's right. Even if you are divorced, you may still be entitled to your ex-spouse's benefits. (We will cover that in our next chapter.)

If you are one of the lucky ones that are entitled to a pension, kudos to you. You are ahead of the game. A pension is guaranteed income that will be paid out to you when you retire. Typically, when you hear about pensions, some of the more common ones are teachers, state and local government workers, union employees, police officers, and firefighters.

If you're not, let's keep going. Remember our pretty, little vehicles? I'm not referring to the Maserati or Porsche. We are talking about IRAs and company-sponsored retirement plans [e.g., 401(k), 403(b), or 457]. If your company offers a retirement plan, please sign up as soon as you are eligible. If you wait, you are wasting precious time. As I mentioned previously, many times companies will match a portion of your contribution, and if that is the case, that is free money in your pocket.

If you do not have a company plan or if you are a business owner or CFO of your household, then an IRA is for you. If you do not have earned income but your spouse does, you can still open up an IRA and make contributions to it every year.

Ladies, you need to do this. Don't rely on your spouse's savings alone. This is another great vehicle in addition to your spouse's where the money grows tax-deferred. When you combine tax-deferral and compounding, the money can accumulate faster.

If you are a business owner—and I was at one point in my life—I can tell you that business owners tend to continually re-invest into their business and don't always think about setting up a retirement plan for themselves. Business owners can put away much more than your typical IRA. Many do not realize that there is actually an IRA specifically designed for small business owners. The most common are SEP and SIMPLE IRA, which are described in chapter 3.

A few things to remember is that compounding is your best friend. Like a snowball rolling down the hill, the value of compounding grows the longer you leave your money in the account. Not having to pay taxes from year to year on your contributions into retirement accounts helps your savings grow even faster. Also make sure you invest and diversify. Work with a professional to help you figure out the most appropriate asset mix between equities, bonds, and cash alternatives.

Another way to build wealth is through investing in real estate. This vehicle can potentially provide an additional source of retirement income when invested in a rental property. Purchasing a property that you can rent out and create positive cash flow is like building your very own pension.

If you are a little late in the game, don't worry. You've come to the right place. I've got you covered, girl! If you haven't put away into a retirement account, whether it be company-sponsored or your own IRA, there is still another tax-deferred vehicle, an annuity. It can also provide you a guaranteed stream of income in retirement. Think of it as a pension/retirement account. Now not all annuities are created equal. Today for the sake of our discussion, I will only cover annuities with a guaranteed lifetime withdrawal benefit.

Here's an example to show how it works. You invest a lump sum, such as $100,000, and depending on the growth and their benefits, once you are ready to start to draw on the income, they guarantee you a certain amount of income for life. Now annuities are complex vehicles, with many different bells and whistles, which means it is important for you to speak to a financial advisor and do your research. This vehicle can also complement your overall retirement strategy even if you do have an IRA or company-sponsored retirement plan [e.g., 401(k)].

So what are some of the things you will need to think about to plan for retirement? Well, it is not any different than what you should be thinking about when just starting out #adulting.

Understand your time horizon. How long until you plan on retiring? Your age and when you plan on retiring are the groundwork for an effective retirement strategy. The longer the time you have (think ten years or more), the higher the risk your portfolio can withstand, which means you can have riskier investments that typically have more growth potential such as stocks.

Determining what your retirement spending needs would be is the next step. That can be a little more difficult to determine when you are much younger, but a rule of thumb is 70 to 80 percent of what your spending habits are before retirement. Of course, depending on lifestyle, it can be more as well.

Figuring out how much assets you have accumulated and how long those assets will last is not just a simple calculation. Very rarely individuals think about the impact of taxes and inflation and how it eats away at your nest egg. That's why it is so important to determine if you are taking on too little or too much risk with your investment strategy. Working with a professional who can ask you all the right questions and help you build out a cash flow analysis is a good start to help you toward your goals.

The bottom line is that it's never too late to start, but you need to take action now. A compromise between reasonable returns, goals, and a desired standard of living is one of the most difficult aspects of designing a detailed retirement plan. Focusing on building a flexible portfolio that can be periodically updated to match changing market conditions and retirement goals is the best approach.

Common Investment Mistakes to Avoid

- Do not make investment decisions based on emotions and not facts.
- Do not choose investments not suited to your goals or investment time horizon.
- Do not react to short-term events and not to long-term trends.
- Do not try to time the market.
- Do not chase a "hot" investment with no basis for your decision.
- Do not allow fees, expenses, and/or commissions to become the major factor in making investment decisions.
- Do not allow fear or greed to drive your investment decisions.

DISCLOSURE

With variable annuities, any withdrawals may be subject to income taxes and, prior to age fifty-nine and a half, a 10 percent federal penalty tax may apply. Withdrawals from annuities will affect both the account value and the death benefit. The investment return and principal value will fluctuate so that an investor's shares, when redeemed, may be worth more or less than their original cost. An annual contingent deferred sales charge (CDSC) may apply.

Before investing, investors should carefully consider the

investment objectives, risks, charges, and expenses of the variable annuity and its underlying investment options. The current contract prospectus and underlying fund prospectuses, which are contained in the same document, provide this and other important information. Please contact your representative or the company to obtain prospectuses. Please read the prospectuses carefully before investing or sending money. Variable annuities are generally considered long-term investments.

STAGE 3
I Don't!

What to Do When It Isn't 'Til Death Do Us Part

CHAPTER TEN

How to Cope with Divorce

Can I afford to live on my own?

Will my kids be okay?

Will my lifestyle change?

So this is the part when all those annoying little things you used to love about them, or let's say tolerated, have now been amplified by a hundred and you are ready for them to go poof and be gone! Yes, all those thoughts are just going through your head, "Siri, how do I make him disappear?" Kidding, but not kidding. The thoughts come with the territory. It's okay. They are just thoughts.

I said, "I do," and then seventeen years later, I decided, "I don't." You certainly never expect going into your marriage thinking that your fairy tale won't work out, but it happens, and it did. I had to make a decision, and although probably one of the hardest decisions I've had to make, when I actually made it, I felt such a weight lifted off my shoulders.

Whether you are the dumper or dumpee—my apologies, I know the visual when you say those words are not very pleasant—divorce is one of the most difficult life transitions anyone can go through, especially when children are involved.

There are all these questions that go through your head. Will my kids be okay? Will I ever find anyone else? Will my lifestyle change? Can I support myself? Or maybe you're saying to yourself, "How dare he do this to me?

It's an emotional roller coaster. You are dealing with a slew of emotions: anger, sadness, despair, defeat, guilt, and sometimes even denial. You replay conversations over and over again. Where did it go wrong? "If I only ..."

Once you get past those and make the decision to move on, which will take time, then comes elation, freedom, living again, a breath of fresh air, the new you! When you have come to accept it, and you come to realize that your happiness is important, then you are ready to move on and take it head-on. It's the most amazing feeling once your head is there. It was my fresh start, my new chapter, I was happy again. I found me again, someone I lost for a very long time.

It's okay to be scared. Anything new is scary regardless of what it is. Parting with a spouse is challenging, both emotionally and financially. And navigating the process requires careful planning to help you answer questions like: What happens to your assets? Where will you live? Will your post-divorce income be enough? How will the divorce impact your family and your financial future?

Divorce can be a lengthy process that may strain your finances and leave you feeling out of control. But with the right planning, you can protect your interests, take charge of your future, and save yourself time and money.

Preparing for this next chapter can seem overwhelming at times, but with informed guidance and preparation, you will be able to better navigate the legal, financial, and emotional issues to come.

When you are dealing with the emotional end of it, this is when you need your tribe—your family and your friends. Don't forget the Kleenex, and a little bit of wine always helps. Everyone is going to offer advice, and sometimes it will be great. Other times you have to block out the noise, but regardless they are there for you.

Surround yourself with positive people; stay away from the negative ones. Sometimes a good cry with your puppy dog helps too. They have an amazing gift of just listening. Hiring a therapist for yourself and kids is great too. It's someone objective who can listen and give you unbiased advice.

Talk to your children. Mine were twelve, ten, and six when my divorce started. I'm not going to lie. It was a difficult conversation, but fast-forward a few years later, my children told me it was the best thing I did. Kids see and feel everything. A toxic environment isn't any good for anyone. As much as you think you are doing the right thing by staying together for the sake of the kids, you need to have an honest conversation with yourself and determine if this is really a healthy environment for them. I came from divorced parents, and they waited until I was off to college. I have to tell you. They waited too long. Kids just want to see their parents happy even if it means separately.

Talk to your children together and be civil in front of them. Let them know that the divorce is not their fault. Also it's very important to not speak badly in front of them about the other spouse. (I know. It's extremely hard not to do.) Don't use your children to get even, and don't confide in your children like they are your best friends. Maintain your role as a parent. I'm only giving you this advice as a mom and my experience. There are a lot of therapists and divorce coaches out there that specialize in children and divorce, and you should certainly look to get one on your team.

The team is very important, along with who you have on it. When you start looking for an attorney, you need to consider whether meditation, collaboration, or using your own attorneys makes the most sense for your situation. When you go see an attorney, it sometimes helps to have family or a friend with you.

Gathering all the financials and making sense of it all can be overwhelming. Hiring a Certified Divorce Financial Analyst/ financial advisor on your team will help you organize all the documents you need and will help you prepare everything your attorney would require. A certified public accountant (CPA) is also an important part of your team. They will help provide you guidance on any tax implications you will have to deal with along the way.

Organizing your paperwork is going to be key. It doesn't matter whether you know what any of the stuff is. Your goal is to get all your paperwork in one place so your attorney, financial advisor, and CPA can help you.

Getting one of those accordion files is a good start. You'll want to create the following labels.

- **Liquid Assets**

  o   Bank accounts
  o   Brokerage accounts
  o   CDs
  o   Money market accounts
  o   Savings bonds
  o   Stock options
  o   Employee stock options (ESOP)
  o   Employee stock purchase plan (ESPP)
  o   Mutual funds
  o   Physical stock certificates
  o   Stocks held at a transfer agent (like ComputerShare)
  o   Business financial statements

- **Real Assets**

  o   Primary home
  o   Second home
  o   Land or buildings
  o   Businesses
  o   Vehicles, boats, and other toys
  o   Timeshares
  o   Collectibles
  o   Jewelry
  o   Art

- **Retirement Assets**

  o Retirement statements: 401(k), 403(b), 457, profit-sharing plans, and retirement savings plans
  o Annuities
  o Individual Retirement Accounts (IRAs)
  o Social Security statements
    ▪ You may be entitled to your ex-spouse's even after divorce.
  o Pension plans
  o Defined benefit plans
  o SEP or SIMPLE IRA
  o Deferred compensation plans
  o Profit-sharing

- **Insurance and Benefits**

  o Life insurance (term, universal, or whole life)
  o Disability insurance
  o Health insurance
  o Dental insurance
  o Vision insurance
  o Long-term care insurance
  o Healthcare savings account (HSA)
  o Flexible spending account (FSA)

- **Liabilities (Debt)**

  o Mortgage
  o Equity line of credit
  o Car loan
  o Personal loans (from friends or family)
  o Credit card debt
  o Student loans
  o Security-based loans
  o Margin balance

- o   Taxes, liens, or judgments owed
- o   Leases

- **Other Miscellaneous Documents**

  - o   Wills
  - o   Trusts
  - o   Power of attorney (POA)
  - o   Healthcare directives
    - ▪   If your spouse is named as your healthcare proxy, you may want to change that as soon as possible; otherwise your life may be in their hands.
  - o   Auto, homeowners, and renters insurance policies
  - o   Marriage certificate
  - o   Prenuptial agreement
  - o   Deeds and titles

Your tax return for the past few years (preferably five) will also help uncover if there are any accounts that you may be missing.

Understanding what your expenses are, is key in planning and negotiating accordingly. Pull out your bank statements, checking accounts, and credit card bills and start making a list of the following:

- Mortgage/rent
- Utilities
- Groceries
- Taxes
- Insurance (property/auto/life/health)
- House/car maintenance
- Transportation
- Credit cards
- Student debt
- Medical/dental/pharmacy
- Child care

- Travel school
- Therapy
- Kids' camps and activities
- Entertainment/vacations
- "Me" maintenance (hair/nails/gym)

Now that you have all your documents in place and have an idea of all your expenses, it's time to figure out what your next chapter will look like financially. Finding a financial advisor/CDFA that specializes in divorce and working with women would be a great next step. They can help you answer some of those questions that are top of mind for you, such as:

- Can I afford to stay in my home?
- How do I know which assets are the best for me to retain?
- What are my options for health insurance?
- What kind of lifestyle can I afford?

You will need to consider more essential questions, although a divorce professional will help you resolve the more significant issues. However, you might want to start thinking about the following items before your meeting:

- If you have children, what are the wishes regarding custody, visitation, and child support?
- Whose health insurance plan should cover the children?
- Do you earn enough money to adequately support yourself, or should alimony be considered?
- Which assets do you really want, and which are you willing to let your spouse keep? (Splitting assets will vary depending on what state you reside in.)
- How do you feel about the family home?
- Will you have enough money to pay outstanding debt on whatever assets you keep?

Once the divorce is finalized, you will have to make sure you update all your beneficiaries, will, trust documents, POA, and health care proxy, if you haven't done so already. In addition, make sure you have adequate insurance for yourself in case of illness or disability.

Also, I can't tell you how many times I have come across women who think their documents have been retitled just because the divorce has been finalized. For some reason, they are under the impression that the court magically does this for them. I also want to add, if a spouse has a complex executive compensation plan, you need to make sure that all the assets have been properly transferred and retitled in your name. Not for nothing, but your ex-spouse isn't going to let you know if you left money behind and didn't take the proper steps to change it into your name. A Financial Professional can help prepare a checklist of the next steps based on your divorce decree. Don't leave the money you are entitled to behind!

Now you are well on your way to taking control of your new chapter, new you, and new financial future. Let's fast-forward and look at your new life. Well, I don't have a crystal ball, but I will share with you what my new life looked like. It's exciting when you start out and you don't have the dreaded "D" word hanging over your head anymore.

For me, it was time to ditch the unhealthy habits that got me through the not-so-pleasant time in my life, and now I got myself onto a health kick. Working out became my sanity, and in turn, I got into the best shape of my life, which made me feel amazing mentally, and physically.

I signed up to every dating app possible. Yes, I did ladies, and I'm not ashamed of it. Well, maybe a little bit. It was actually very entertaining. There are certainly a lot of characters on those.

Ladies, beware! If they say they are five-foot-eleven, they are probably more like five-foot-six. If they say they are forty, add five to seven years to it. If they say they are a consultant, they probably do not have a job.

I got so frustrated, so I wrote on my profile I am five-foot-six and I love to wear my heels.

Finally, I had one guy who didn't even have anything written on his profile, just pictures with his kids. Typically I wouldn't go for guys who don't have anything written about themselves, but this one guy had one little sentence, "I'm six-foot-four, and you could wear your heels."

Yes, ladies, he wrote it for me! It took a lot of frogs to finally meet my prince, and I did. It was love at first sight. He was tall and dark with his dreamy-brown eyes. The best part is that he treats me like a queen!

So if you are ever feeling discouraged, don't. Enjoy your "me" time, your friends, and your family. Go out and try something you never did before. And go meet new people. You never know what kind of friendships you will develop.

Swipe away, ladies! If you don't know what I mean now, you'll know once you get on those dating apps. Like, don't like. Like, like, don't like.

It's okay if you meet a few weirdos here and there. Just be smart and be safe. Eventually I met my forever weirdo I fell in love with, but it took time. So keep swiping, ladies!

CHAPTER ELEVEN

Your Very Own Brady Bunch

Swipe ...

"The Brady Bunch, the Brady Bunch, that's how we all became, the Brady Bunch."

(Badabumpbumpbump)

Yes, I got my very own Brady Bunch by swiping right. Honestly, I didn't think I would meet someone so quickly that I connected with, but I did, and here we are five years later. We have a blended family of six kids. I have two boys and a girl, and he has three girls. Yes, I went from one daughter to four.

It was quite the adjustment, especially for my ears. I don't know if it is just me, but girls are way louder than boys, and they tend to scream in their highest-pitched voice all the time, not to mention just about all of them started to experience different stages of puberty when we became a big happy family. I know. You feel for me.

Lucky for us, our kids loved each other, and they all became best friends. We were fortunate that they were all around the same ages, so they really blended well right from the get-go. However, the adjustment from three to six kids certainly wasn't a walk in the park.

I think what's on most people's minds is, "How do you blend the two families together?" You know your kids best. You have to feel them out. I recommend baby steps.

For me, the timing felt right, and I was driving one day with the kids. I started telling them that I have a new friend, and my youngest, who was around seven, asked, "Who's your friend, Mom? Jake from State Farm?"

And we all bursted out laughing. That moment right there broke the ice. It went from a very serious conversation to all of us just cracking up, and then I proceeded to say, "Well, it's not Jake from State Farm, but you can call him Chris from State Farm."

Then of course I just started to tell them about his girls and how they were the same ages and talked about all the things they had in common. My daughter was actually really excited.

She said, "I always wanted sisters." And that's what they became, sisters.

My youngest son didn't really have too much input, other than Jake from State Farm. My oldest son was really into motocross racing, and so was Chris. He used to race motocross, so I just told him all about that. Although they were nervous at first about meeting everyone, they were all kind of excited. Of course I didn't introduce them until I knew we were serious about each other.

I guess the best way to describe blending a family is to remember bringing your first baby home. You were completely overwhelmed and certain you were doing the whole parenting thing wrong. Then all of a sudden when your family and friends started telling you their stories about motherhood, you realized you weren't alone. This happens for blended families too. We struggle and struggle, and then we realize we are not the only ones going through this.

They really should have support groups for this. Hmm, I bet you they do. Woman Warriors of Blended Families? Ha, I just made that up. Maybe I need to start one up? Regardless, I didn't think about it then, but perhaps you should if you are considering this next step.

Bringing two families under one roof can be quite challenging. My house is crazy all the time. Quiet? What's quiet? I'm not sure I know that word anymore. Can I tell you how much teenagers actually consume in food? They don't stop eating. My grocery bill more than doubled, not to mention having to cook for six kids. Who doesn't like what? This one took too much and didn't leave enough for the other. Yes, welcome to my home.

Me time? You're lucky if you ever find your own space anywhere else in the house other than your bedroom. Yes, I spent a ton of time in my bedroom. With six kids, they basically took over my house. When you thought you were outnumbered with three kids, just imagine six.

About 75 percent of those who divorce will eventually remarry (Parents.com), and a blended family can be complicated. Your disciplining styles are different, not to mention actually having to discipline your stepchildren. I was used to my kids doing things a certain way, and when his didn't, it would be frustrating for me. So it took time to adjust. It took many conversations with my other half and more conversations with our kids, but we got through it.

Adding your ex into the mix can further complicate things. In my case, my ex did not want my new spouse to replace his role. He didn't want him disciplining them or the kids going to him for advice. It was a little bit of a tug-of-war at the beginning. Eventually he learned to accept him and realized that having another individual who genuinely cared for his children was a good thing, not bad.

There comes a time when everything does eventually fall into place, and it did for us with a little time and patience. Now that we have our two oldest kids off to college, the noise has lessened, and I can't believe I am saying it, but I miss it. I love our big, blended family. I love our craziness and our mess (well, maybe not the mess), but I've gotten used to it, and I wouldn't have it any other way.

So how do you plan mentally, emotionally, and financially for your blended family? Lots of wine, more wine, and more wine. No, that is not the answer, not the answer to anything. It's with a lot of patience and communication with your spouse, kids, and even your tribe. My sister and friends talked me through a bunch of meltdowns, put things into perspective for me, and helped me get through the adjustment period.

Now let's talk money. Dealing with finances is difficult for any marriage. If you add in children, money becomes even more complicated when it comes to second marriages. In my case, I struggled with what I leave to my kids versus what I leave to my current spouse. Something to consider is additional life insurance on each other. Your assets can potentially provide for your spouse while insurance proceeds will provide children an inheritance.

If you have minor children or estate taxes are a concern, establishing an irrevocable trust to buy life insurance for your children's benefit as an alternative to you or your children owning policies on your life is an option.

Remember your team. Having a trust and estate attorney on your team is very important to help you understand the different options available out there to protect you and your family. There is no wrong or right answer. It's just what makes the most sense for you as an individual and your family needs.

Often there are also income tax ramifications that should be discussed with your CPA, and you need to consider them when remarrying. Having a discussion about child support and alimony is a must. Many times alimony may be reduced or stopped upon remarriage.

There's something else to consider, and this only pertains to certain states, particularly community property states. If your ex-spouse remarries, the new spouse is not responsible for providing for your children financially, in most cases. In certain situations, however, the new spouse's income may become part of community property shared with your ex-spouse, and it can be considered in the child support calculation (Institute for Divorce Financial Analyst). So if you are considering getting remarried, you need to understand all the financial facts and how you will be impacted. Always have your team of professionals and seek their guidance before making any life-impacting decisions like marriage.

If you are thinking about adopting your stepchildren, think twice. You're unlikely to be required to make child support payments for a stepchild, but if you adopt them and divorce again, you may be responsible for child support payments.

To play it on the safer side, a prenuptial agreement will spell out each spouse's rights, duties, and obligations during marriage. It will specify what happens if you separate or divorce or if one passes away. And most importantly, it will protect the legal rights of both spouses and any of the children involved.

Remember, you are not alone. Communicate honestly with your partner about expectations and focus on the well-being of your family as a whole. Be kind to yourself. Celebrate your success. And if you can get your very own Alice, do it!

STAGE 4

The Golden Girls

CHAPTER TWELVE

Achieve Your Financial Dream

Where will I live?

Who's going to change that light bulb for me?

Who will take care of me?

They say the seventies are the new sixties, fifties are the new forties, and grey is the new blonde. In my eyes, *The Golden Girls* are the new *Sex in the City* girls. You know why? Because we are getting younger and younger and living longer and longer. Thanks to great supplements, modern medicine, a few nips and tucks, and technology, we can look and feel fabulous and live it up way more in the golden years than our parents did.

Retirement was once a clear line between working and

not working. That is not the case anymore. Technology is offering new options and flexibility. We can work well into our golden years if we choose to. Even the way we live in our homes has changed dramatically with technology. Tech can help with chores but also transform our homes into a helper, companion, and a caregiver. We even have apps that monitor our health and can inform our family members of any concerns. In addition, we now have grocery delivery, Uber, and services to help us around the house, not to mention doctors on demand.

Planning for this stage in our life is so different than what we have always been taught. It's no longer retirement planning; it is longevity planning. It is now reasonable to begin looking at one hundred years of life as the new normal.

My girlfriends and I made a pact that once we are alone in our golden years, we will all move in together and finish out our happily ever after. We all have our tribe, the one that always has an opinion and gives too much advice, the one that shops too much and has every trendiest outfit that exists, the one that is always on some sort of fad diet or magic pill, the party animal, and the know-it-all. But you love them regardless, and they will forever be by your side, 'til death do us part.

So as we enter this stage of life, what are some of the things we need to think about? Are you going to downsize or upsize your living arrangement? Retirement community or assisted living? Warmer or cooler climate? Proximity to family? Moving in with family? City or suburbs? How will you get around?

The beauty of these days is everything that can help us live an independent and fabulous life at this stage is available to us literally at our fingertips. There's Dog Vacay so we can go travel the world with our besties and know that our darling little pooches are being taken care of in a home environment. Hop Skip Drive are individuals with caregiving experience that can drive you around to all your errands. Silver Ride will even take you to your grandkids' ballgame or the Yankees game if that is what you are up for, even if mobility is an issue for you. I read about this contact lens that you wear, and if you need to fix something, it shows you how to fix it through your vision. Even if you are trying to walk somewhere, it will give you step-by-step directions through your lenses. Fascinating, isn't it? I wonder if this will be the answer to cognitive issues in the future.

Well, with us living so much longer, on our own, and having these resources available to us, a hefty price tag will come along with it if you want to have the options.

So what will your golden years look like, and how do we plan for it? At this point, I hope you understand the importance of starting to save as much as you can, as early as possible. Tax deferral is your friend, which means the more you can put away into retirement vehicles, like your company 401(k)/403(b) or IRA, the better off you are.

If you are flexible with moving, look into states with a favorable tax code. Your money will go further with lower-taxed states such as Delaware being number one and then Hawaii, District of Columbia, Wyoming, Nevada, Colorado, South Carolina, Arizona, Arkansas, and Tennessee (Kiplinger.com).

According to (money.usnews), some other favorable states from a tax perspective are Alabama, Alaska, Florida, Illinois, Mississippi, New Hampshire, Pennsylvania, South Dakota, Texas, and Washington.

The most important thing you will want to plan for in your golden years is if you need long-term care down the line. It's one of the largest expenses that come with aging and living longer.

Whether it be a nursing home, assisted living, home modifications, at-home care, or some adult day care, long-term care insurance helps cover the cost of assistance with your daily living tasks when an illness or accident prevents you from being able to perform them. This includes bathing, dressing, eating, and mobility.

When it comes to long-term care, there is no one-size-fits-all. You don't want to buy a costly policy that has benefits you don't end up using. On the other hand, you don't want too little insurance either.

When shopping for long-term care, understanding the different types will help you determine the right fit. Use-it-or-lose-it will provide you with the largest benefit for the lowest cost, but if you never use it, you don't get a return of premium or anything. Similar to car or property insurance, it's just there to protect you, but you may never have the need for it.

The next type is called asset-based. Most of the time it's a lump sum or one-time payment, or some companies will allow you to pay it over a term of ten years. With this type of long-term care, if you pass without using it, the death benefit to your beneficiaries would typically be what you put into the policy in premiums. With the asset-based plans, you get a little less of a benefit, and the cost is a little more than your use-it-or-lose-it plans.

The last type is, life insurance with the long-term care rider. With this type of policy, if you never use the policy, it comes with a death benefit to your beneficiaries. This type of policy is the most expensive, with the least long-term care benefit, but in turn, it does have the greatest death benefit. When shopping around for these policies, it is very important to price out the benefits versus the cost.

They say the best time to shop around for these policies is between ages fifty-five to sixty-five because you can be turned down for pre-existing conditions, and the younger and healthier you are, the less expensive the policy will be.

Not only is it important to plan for ourselves, but it is important to plan for our parents who are entering this stage. I'm in the sandwich generation where I have young kids and my parents are in their golden years. If we do not properly set up our parents, then the burden will be on us. I couldn't imagine while I have kids in college to also have an additional expense of taking care of my parents. We as the sandwich generation do not want that additional financial burden, and we certainly do not want to become that for our children.

Now all you *Sex in the City* ladies, go rock the world! You have the tools to be financially independent and live your best life!

DISCLOSURE

Guarantees are based on the claims-paying ability of the issuing company. Long-term care insurance or asset-based long-term care insurance products may not be suitable for all investors. Surrender charges may apply for early withdrawals and, if made prior to age fifty-nine and a half, may be subject to a 10 percent federal tax penalty in addition to any gains being taxed as ordinary income. Please consult with a licensed financial professional when considering your insurance options.

CONCLUSION

I Wanna Hold Your Hand

As we walk through this life journey together as women, I want to hold your hand because we as women are capable of anything we put our mind to. I can tell you that I am surrounded by the most amazing, strongest, most loving, and smartest women I know. They are my mom, my sister, and my best friends.

I've seen them struggle, face adversity, deal with the unthinkable, and continue to fight and get ahead, no matter what. As determined and bright as they are, for some reason, finances intimidate them, making them feel inadequate or ignorant.

We all come from different walks of life. Growing up, I came from nothing, but what I learned from my childhood is to work as hard as I can. I was taught that there will be roadblocks and I just need to push through them. I did, and I will continue to do so.

I am grateful for this path I was put on and the knowledge I have acquired through my life and career. I wrote this book for all the special women in my life and every other women that for some reason or another thinks this is too hard. I'm here to tell you that it is not that hard. You have the tools now. You have my hand and my guidance. I'm here to answer your questions.

Let's be a voice for each other, our children, and our future. Now get to work, my ladies. This is your chapter now!